W9-ADL-338

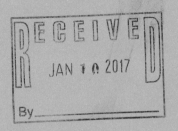
RECEIVED
JAN 1 0 2017
By_____

HAYNER PLD/DOWNTOWN
OVERDUES .10 PER DAY. MAXIMUM
FINE COST OF ITEM. LOST OR
DAMAGED ITEM ADDITIONAL $5.00
SERVICE CHARGE

HaTCHiNG CHiCKS iN ROOM 6

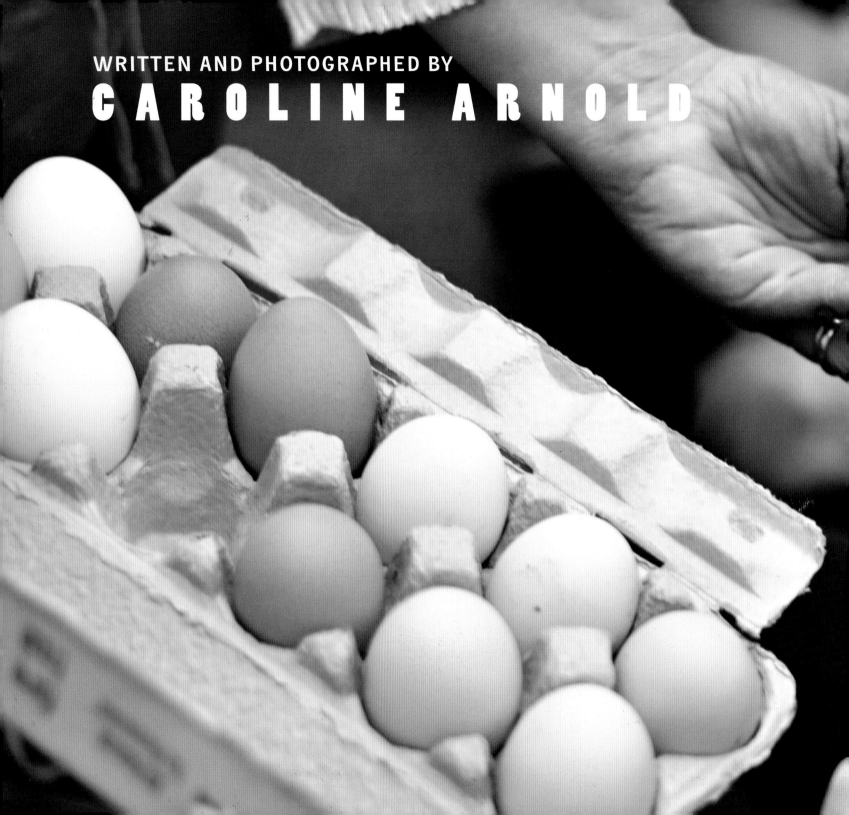

WRITTEN AND PHOTOGRAPHED BY
CAROLINE ARNOLD

HATCHING CHICKS IN ROOM 6

Charlesbridge

636.507
ARN

3481710

MRS. BEST KEEPS CHICKENS IN HER BACKYARD.

Every day the hens lay eggs. Every day Mrs. Best collects the eggs for her family to eat. But today Mrs. Best is bringing the eggs to school.

Many chicken eggs are white. Eggshells can also be brown, green, blue, or speckled. The color depends on the type of chicken.

Mrs. Best is a teacher. The children in her class are learning about chicks and how they grow from eggs.

A hen lays her eggs in a nest. If she sits on them for twenty-one days, the eggs hatch into chicks.

A hen keeps her eggs warm and moist and turns them with her feet and beak.

An eggshell protects the growing chick inside.

The children put the eggs in an incubator.
They look through the plastic cover and
watch the eggs move on the turning rack.

Water drips into the incubator and makes the air moist. This keeps the lining inside the eggs from drying out.

A heater keeps the air warm.

A motor moves the rack. This turns the eggs and keeps the growing chicks from getting stuck on one side of the shell.

The eggs went into the incubator on Day 1.
They will hatch on Day 21. While the children
wait for the eggs to hatch, they count the
days and learn about chickens and eggs.

hen

A chicken's life cycle begins with a fertile egg. You need a hen and rooster to make a fertile egg. A hen is a female chicken. A rooster is a male chicken.

A chick starts growing when the egg goes into the incubator. Each day the chick grows a little bigger.

rooster

The skin on top of a chicken's head is called a comb. The flap of skin under the chin is a wattle. Roosters have bigger combs and wattles than hens do.

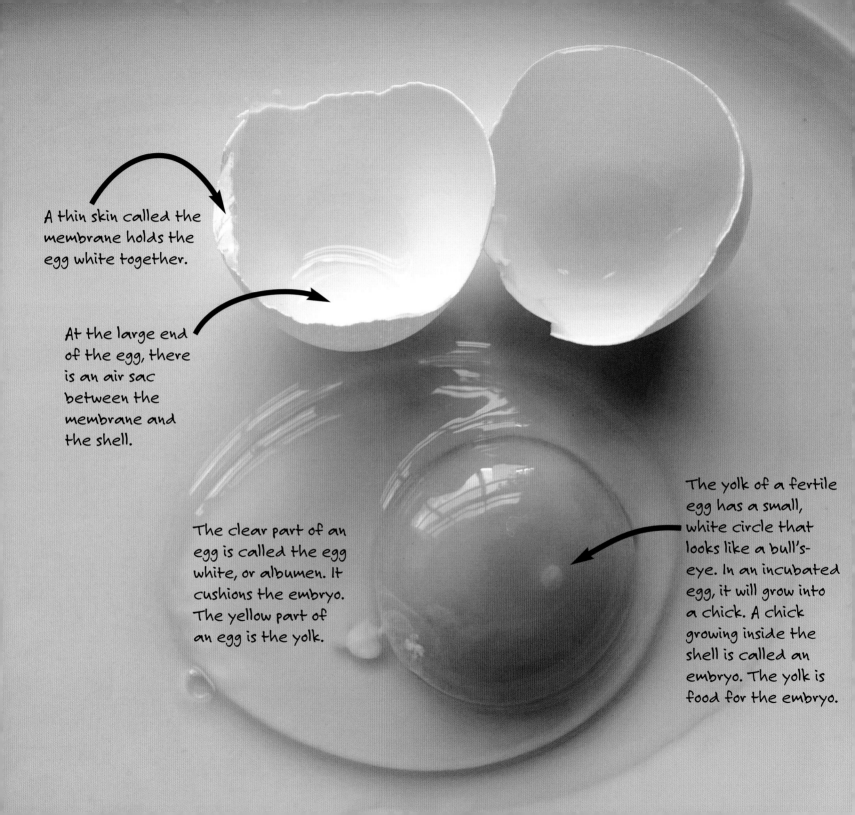

A thin skin called the membrane holds the egg white together.

At the large end of the egg, there is an air sac between the membrane and the shell.

The clear part of an egg is called the egg white, or albumen. It cushions the embryo. The yellow part of an egg is the yolk.

The yolk of a fertile egg has a small, white circle that looks like a bull's-eye. In an incubated egg, it will grow into a chick. A chick growing inside the shell is called an embryo. The yolk is food for the embryo.

On Day 12 Mrs. Best takes an egg out of the incubator and puts it on top of a bright light. Then she turns off the lights in the room to make it dark. A shadow shows the shape of the chick inside the shell. Thin red lines show blood vessels that are bringing food from the yolk to the chick.

By the time the chick is done growing, it will fill the whole shell except for the air sac at the end.

Shining a light through an egg is called candling.

The dark part is the shadow of the chick's body.

On Day 18 Mrs. Best shuts off the motor that turns the eggs in the incubator. Now the eggs must stay still. The chicks inside the eggs are almost done growing.

The chicks turn inside their shells to face up as they hatch.

On Day 20 the chicks poke a hole into the air sac inside their shells. They breathe air for the first time.

Peep, peep, they call.

The children listen carefully. They can hear the chicks calling.

Just one more day until they hatch!

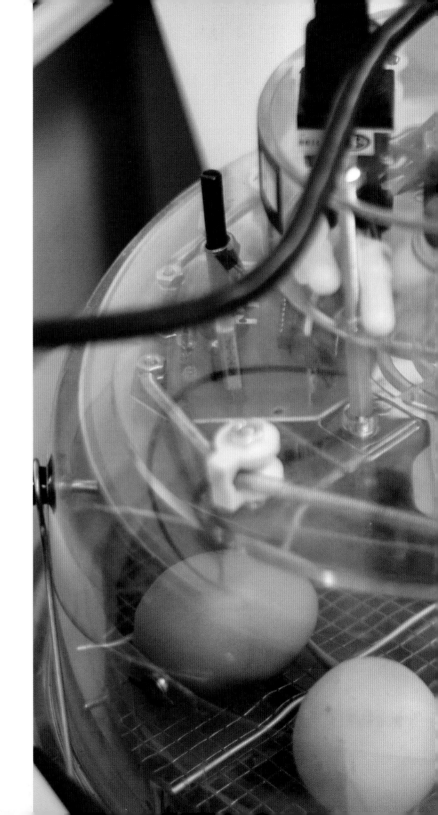

Day 21. Hatching day!

In the morning the children see small holes in some of the eggs. Soon other eggs have holes, too. Each chick has a sharp knob called an egg tooth on the top of its beak. The chick taps it against the shell to make the first hole, called a pip.

An eggshell is strong. It is hard to break open. The chick rests a while after pipping.

Then it starts to tap again.

Most chicks hatch twelve to eighteen hours after they pip, but the time for some is longer or shorter.

pip

The chick slowly pecks a circle
around the inside of its shell.
Little by little, the shell begins
to crack. It is like unzipping
a zipper.

The chick is curled up like a ball inside its shell. It lies on its back and pushes with its head and feet. Finally, many hours after pipping, the chick pushes one more time and the shell pops open.

THE CHICK HAS HATCHED!

One by one, the eggs hatch. Some chicks are yellow. Some are white or tan. One of them is black.

Hatching is hard work. The new chicks are tired. Their feathers are wet. Their legs wobble when they stand up. They lie down and rest while their feathers dry.

All the chicks stay in the incubator overnight.

There are more than one hundred types, or breeds, of chickens. Each breed has its own colors and patterns of feathers. Mrs. Best's chicks are a mix of several different breeds.

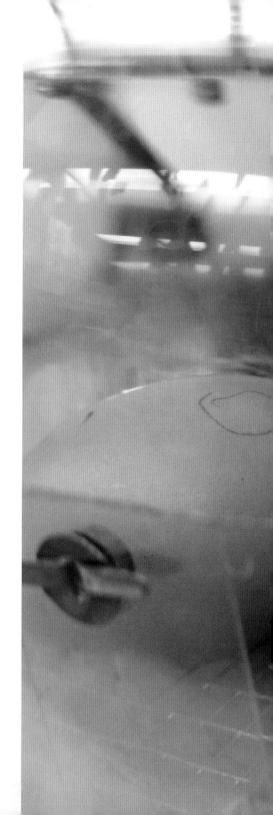

The egg tooth is at the end of the chick's beak. In a day or two, it will dry up and fall off. The chick does not need it anymore.

When the children come to school the next morning, the chicks are hopping around inside the incubator.

Peep, peep! they call.

Now the chicks look fluffy. Their feathers have dried. They are ready to go to a brood box.

A chick's fluffy feathers are called down. They help keep the chick warm.

The new chicks are hungry and thirsty. Mrs. Best moves them from the incubator to the brood box.

The chicks have food and water in the brood box. A light keeps them warm, and they have plenty of room to move around.

The chicks still need a lot of rest. When they are not eating or drinking, they snuggle together.

A group of chicks that hatch together is called a clutch. When a hen hatches a clutch of chicks, she keeps them warm under her wings. Chicks know how to peck for food and drink water as soon as they hatch.

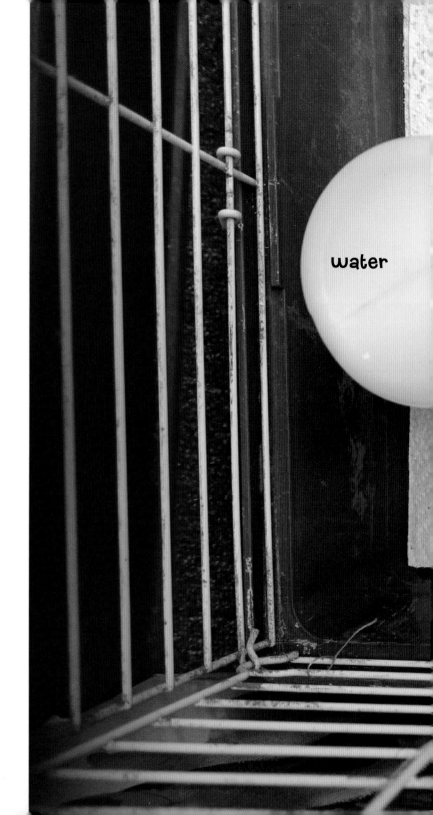

water

food

Pebbles keep the chicks from falling in during the first few days after they hatch.

ear

Chick mash is a mixture of corn, grains, vegetables, and nutrients. It is ground into small pieces just the right size for the chicks to eat.

Each day, the chicks grow bigger and stronger. Now they are six days old. Mrs. Best brings some of them out of the brood box. If the children sit very still, the chicks will eat food from their hands.

Now the chicks are ten days old. Their legs are getting stronger. Feathers are growing on their wings and tails. Tiny combs are beginning to appear on their heads. They are big enough to hop out of the cage by themselves.

The children have named each of the chicks. The most adventurous one is Cookie.

Mrs. Best shows the children how to hold the chicks. Their feathers feel soft, but their feet tickle.

Chickens are birds. They have feathers and wings. But they don't fly very well.

Chickens do not have teeth. They eat small pebbles and dirt to help grind their food into small pieces so it can be digested.

The chicks are now three weeks old. They are big enough to spend the day in an outside pen.

The chicks have food and water in their pen. They scratch the ground with their feet, looking for small plants, seeds, and insects. For a special treat the children give them mealworms.

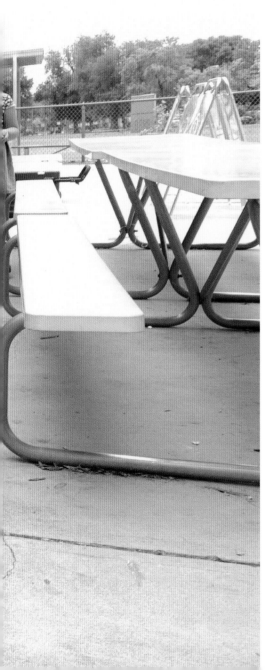

IT IS TIME FOR THE CHILDREN TO SAY GOOD-BYE TO THE CHICKS.

The chicks are nearly a month old. Mrs. Best will take them back to her house, where they will join her other chickens.

The chicks will finish growing in a few months. In about five months the roosters will be able to crow. The hens will start laying eggs. Perhaps next year some of their eggs will come back to school and hatch into new chicks.

CHICK QUESTIONS

When you eat an egg, are you eating a baby chick?

Most eggs that you buy at the grocery store are not fertile. They will never grow into chicks, even if you put them in an incubator.

Why do some eggs not hatch even after they have been incubated?

Sometimes the chick does not develop properly or is too weak to hatch. Typically, between 50 and 80 percent of incubated eggs hatch. Mrs. Best's class incubated sixteen eggs in two incubators, and fourteen hatched.

Why do all eggs in a clutch hatch on the same day?

Even when eggs are laid on different days, the chicks do not begin to develop until the eggs are incubated. Eggs remain fertile for up to ten days after they are laid.

How can you tell if a new chick will be a hen or rooster?

You can't. Male and female chicks look alike when they hatch. As they grow older their appearance and behavior show whether they are hens or roosters.

Do chickens make good pets?

No. They are smelly and noisy and usually not very tame. Chickens do best living outdoors in a chicken coop. Before you hatch eggs, make sure that you have a home for the chicks to go to.

CHICK VOCABULARY

air sac: the air space at the large end of an egg.

albumen: the white part of an egg.

beak: the hard covering over a bird's mouth.

blood vessel: a tube that brings food to an embryo.

breed: a particular type of animal or plant.

brood box: a container that keeps new chicks warm.

candling: shining a light through an eggshell.

chick: a young chicken.

clutch: a group of chicks that hatch together.

comb: the flap of skin at the top of a chicken's head. Like the wattle, it helps keep the chicken warm or cool.

down: a new chick's fluffy feathers.

egg tooth: the hard knob at the end of a chick's beak.

embryo: an animal in the earliest stages of development.

hatch: when a chick breaks open its egg.

hen: an adult female chicken.

incubator: a device that keeps eggs warm and moist for hatching.

membrane: the thin skin that lines an eggshell.

pip: the first hole a chick makes in its shell; also, the process of making the first hole in the shell.

rooster: an adult male chicken.

wattle: the flap of skin under a chicken's chin. Like the comb, it helps keep the chicken warm or cool.

yolk: the yellow part of an egg.

CHICKS ONLINE

Chicken Embryo Development
https://www.youtube.com/watch?v=PedajVADLGw
Animation of day-by-day embryo development and hatching.

Chick Hatching
https://www.youtube.com/watch?v=tof5b1Qs_OE
Video of chick hatching.

Egg and Embryo Development
http://www.enchantedlearning.com/subjects/birds/info/chicken/egg.shtml
Details of egg formation and chart of embryo development.

Hatching Eggs in the Classroom
http://oaktrust.library.tamu.edu/bitstream/handle/1969.1/87721/pdf_614.pdf
A teacher's guide that includes tips for storing and incubating eggs, a troubleshooting guide, and an incubator data chart.

How to Incubate and Hatch Chicks
http://www.backyardchickens.com/a/how-to-incubate-hatch-eggs-just-21-days-from-egg-to-chicken
Practical advice for hatching chicks.

FURTHER READING ABOUT CHICKS

Chicks and Chickens by Gail Gibbons (Holiday House, 2003)
All about the behavior and development of chicks and chickens.

From Egg to Chicken by Anita Ganeri (Heinemann, 2006)
Life cycle of the chicken, illustrated with photographs.

Tillie Lays an Egg by Terry Golson, photographs by Ben Fink (Scholastic, 2009)
Fictional story about a chicken who lays her eggs everywhere but in the nest box.

Who You Callin' Chicken? by Thea Feldman, photographs by Stephen Green-Armytage (Abrams, 2003)
Photographs of the amazing variety of chicken breeds.

ACKNOWLEDGMENTS

I thank Jennifer Best and her kindergarten students at Haynes Charter for Enriched Studies, Los Angeles, California, for sharing their chick-hatching experience with me. The children's enthusiasm was contagious as they learned about chickens and eggs and cared for the growing chicks. I am extremely grateful to Jennifer for her wealth of knowledge about hatching chicks in the classroom, for introducing me to her flock at home, and for being my expert reader. I couldn't have done this book without her. The fourteen chicks who are the stars of this book—Allen, Ariel, Anna, Batman, Cookies and Cream (called Cookie), Elsa, Joey, Lucy, Lulu, Marshmallow, Maya, Oreo, Roxie, and Summer— are now adult chickens. It was a remarkable journey watching them hatch and grow.

Dedicated to Jennifer Best, her students, and their families

Copyright © 2017 by Caroline Arnold
Silhouetted egg photographs on pages 5, 6, 11, 14, 16, 20, 22, 24, 27,
    30, and 33 copyright © by Cloud7Days/Shutterstock.com
All rights reserved, including the right of reproduction in whole
or in part in any form. Charlesbridge and colophon are registered
trademarks of Charlesbridge Publishing, Inc.

Published by Charlesbridge
85 Main Street
Watertown, MA 02472
(617) 926-0329
www.charlesbridge.com

Library of Congress Cataloging-in-Publication Data
Names: Arnold, Caroline, author.
Title: Hatching chicks in room 6/Caroline Arnold.
Description: Watertown, MA : Charlesbridge, [2017] | Description based on
    print version record and CIP data provided by publisher; resource not
    viewed.
Identifiers: LCCN 2015048466 (print) | LCCN 2015044368 (ebook) |
    ISBN 9781607349914 (ebook) | ISBN 9781607349921 (ebook pdf) |
    ISBN 9781580897358 (reinforced for library use)
Subjects: LCSH: Chicks—Juvenile literature. | Chickens—Juvenile literature. |
    Eggs—Juvenile literature.
Classification: LCC SF498.4 (print) | LCC SF498.4 .A76 2017 (ebook) | DDC
    636.507—dc23
LC record available at http://lccn.loc.gov/2015048466

Printed in China
(hc) 10 9 8 7 6 5 4 3 2 1

Display type set in Swung Note by PintassilgoPrints; Family Dog Fat
    by Pizzadude.dk; and Poplar by Barbara Lind
Text type set in Jesterday by Jelloween Foundry
Color separations by Colourscan Print Co Pte Ltd, Singapore
Printed by 1010 Printing International Limited in Huizhou, Guangdong, China
Production supervision by Brian G. Walker
Designed by Susan Mallory Sherman